BEASTWORLD

TERRIFYING MONSTERS AND MYTHICAL BEASTS

S. A. Caldwell

SCHOLASTIC
www.scholastic.com

CONTENTS

Throughout the centuries, much has been written of the strange and fabulous beasts that inhabit the far reaches of our world. Legends tell of terrifying creatures with human faces and savage jaws; of spine-chilling monsters that lie in wait for unwary travelers; of enormous water serpents that rise from the deep; and of majestic bird-beasts that soar across the skies.

What exactly are these magical creatures that are so often dismissed as "nonsense," yet clearly visible to those who dare to see? In my long career as a monster hunter, I have crossed frozen mountain ranges, searched vast and barren deserts, and ventured to the murky ocean depths in search of evidence. However, as you will see, fantastic beasts are to be found in the most ordinary of places, too.

As all monster hunters know, the writings of past ages must be studied carefully for clues. It is clear that some legendary creatures, such as the ferocious Minotaur or the headless giants known as the Blemmyes, are now extinct. I also discovered that some creatures assumed to be "mythical"—for example, the fearsome Cerberus of Greek legend or the terrifying bogeyman that stalks the dreams of children—are anything but imaginary.

Within these pages, you will find astonishing evidence gathered from around the world. Magnificent claw specimens, dagger-sharp teeth, and shimmering scales from a variety of beasts are all displayed, along with the remarkable tales of how they came to be found.

I hope this book will show you that, within the natural world, all is not what it seems. It is up to each of us to open our eyes, to look beyond the ordinary, and to discover the extraordinary.

S. A. Caldwell

The Ancient Guild of Beast Research

A World of Monsters

LOOK AROUND YOU, FOR THE WORLD TEEMS
WITH AN ABUNDANCE OF INCREDIBLE BEASTS!
RARELY SEEN AND TOO OFTEN DISMISSED
AS NONSENSE, MONSTERS MAY BE FOUND
IN THE MOST ORDINARY AND
EXTRAORDINARY OF PLACES.

Monster Realms

From frozen mountain peaks to murky ocean depths, and from vast deserts to secluded forests, monsters make their homes in an astonishing variety of places. Fantastic beasts may be spotted in the most ordinary of situations, too, for they inhabit the woods, rivers, and skies around us. However, to catch sight of a monster is still a rare and wonderful thing; only those who truly open their eyes will be lucky enough ever to glimpse one.

Monster Variety

Like creatures of the natural world, a monster's body features are perfectly suited to its habitat. For example, the majestic griffin—part eagle and part lion—makes its home in mountainous regions. This sure-footed beast is able to clamber nimbly over rough terrain, but it is equally at home soaring through the skies in search of jewels and other treasures. In Australia, the man-eating bunyip has nostrils on top of its head, allowing it to lurk just beneath the surface of swamps and creeks. This beast's long, curved tusks are vital for hauling its heavy body onto dry land, as well as for "hooking" unfortunate passersby.

This rugged mountain landscape, with its freshwater stream and wide open sky, is undoubtedly home to many fantastic beasts.

A troll's woodland lair

A dragon's desert shelter

These beast tracks from around the world include the clawed footprints of a baby snow dragon (bottom right) and the unmistakable jungle track of a man-eating manticore (right center).

BEASTS OF THE WORLD

As with animals of the natural world, some beasts are found only in certain regions, while others have adapted to live in many different environments. This map shows where in the world particular beasts are most commonly observed, although these creatures may well have spread to other areas. For example, the majestic hippogriff almost certainly has its roots in ancient Greece, though different species may be found in North Africa and the Americas.

1. Bigfoot—*North America and Canada*
2. Bogeyman—*North America and worldwide*
3. Sea serpent of Cape Ann—*Massachusetts, North America*
4. Zombie—*Haiti and worldwide*
5. Chupacabra—*Puerto Rico and other parts of the Americas*
6. Kraken—*North Atlantic Ocean*
7. Loch Ness Monster—*Scotland*
8. Kelpie—*Scotland and northern Europe*
9. Gryndylow—*Great Britain and northern Europe*
10. Black Dog—*Great Britain and worldwide*
11. Troll—*Scandinavia and worldwide*
12. Garm—*Norway*
13. Harpies—*Southern Europe*
14. Cockatrice—*Europe*
15. Dragons—*Europe, Asia, and worldwide*
16. Scylla—*Strait of Messina (between Italy and Sicily)*
17. Sirens—*Mediterranean islands*
18. Gorgon—*Unidentified Mediterranean island*
19. Minotaur—*(Ancient) Greece*
20. Hydra—*Greece*
21. Cerberus—*Greece*
22. Hippogriff—*Greece and mountainous regions worldwide*
23. Griffin—*Greece and mountainous regions worldwide*
24. Chimera—*Turkey and Greece*
25. Ammut—*Egypt*
26. Roc—*African plains*
27. Vampires—*Eastern Europe and worldwide*
28. Werewolf—*Russia and worldwide*
29. Yeti—*The Himalayas*
30. Manticore—*Asian jungle regions*
31. Nue—*Japan*
32. Yowie—*Australia*
33. Bunyip—*Australia*

NORTH AMERICA

1.

2.

3.

4.

5.

PACIFIC OCEAN

ATLANTIC OCEAN

SOUTH AMERICA

MONSTER TRACKING

Above all, a monster hunter requires a good eye for detail and endless patience. Indeed, it is often necessary to spend long hours hidden away in remote and uncomfortable locations, waiting and watching for the tiniest of clues. As well as persistence, a range of basic equipment is essential for beast-tracking success.

An Arctic beast hunter dressed for freezing conditions.

A monster hunter never travels without the means to record tracks and other evidence accurately.

This ancient chest contains cockatrice scales gathered in the fifteenth century.

Field notes

A right paw — but from what beast?

A small camera is vital for capturing photos and moving images.

MAGICAL CHARMS

Monsters rarely follow the laws of the known natural world, and it may be necessary to use tried-and-tested charms when dealing with unwelcome behavior, or attempting to lure a beast from its lair. Some of these spells will be detailed on the following pages. It is, however, advisable for beginners to learn the following chant, which may be used to calm an angry beast:

Binoculars are essential for viewing beasts from a safe distance.

Many beasts, and particularly those of a supernatural nature, are best observed under cover of darkness.

Oh wondrous beast, pray hear this charm
I am your friend and mean no harm
Oh, stay in sight! Do not take flight!
Spare me from your claws and bite!

Vials are required for gathering samples.

A jungle shelter built from sticks allows safe beast-viewing.

Jars are helpful to preserve larger specimens.

Unidentified tentacle
Cambodia

Tracking ocean-dwelling beasts requires deep-sea diving skills.

Beasts of the Earth

From vast mountain ranges to dark, silent forests where few would ever dare to tread, many strange and wonderful creatures inhabit the far-flung corners of our world.

MOUNTAIN AND FOREST BEASTS

A variety of beasts make their homes in dark, silent forests, or high up in mountainous regions. Tracking such monsters can prove challenging, as it requires courage and good survival skills to venture to such remote regions. Some of the hardest beasts to study are trolls, because they make their lairs in deep forest burrows or black mountain caves. These hideous creatures avoid daylight at all costs, since the sun's rays will turn them to stone. By night, trolls rampage through the wilderness in search of prey, pouncing upon any human they chance to encounter.

Travelers exploring remote regions are easy prey for greedy trolls!

MONSTER APES

The vast Himalayan Mountains of Asia are home to one of the world's most mysterious monsters—the yeti. For centuries, terrified inhabitants have reported seeing giant footprints in the snow, and many claim to have glimpsed a huge, ape-like figure moving across the icy landscape. Bigfoot, a similar ape-monster, stalks the wilderness regions of North America and Canada. Although secretive in nature, this beast seems to enjoy playing tricks on humans. On the other hand, the Australian yowie avoids people at all costs, although it can be incredibly fierce if cornered.

Fur from an Australian yowie.

THE BIGFOOT

I first set eyes on the creature known as bigfoot when I was still an apprentice to the great monster hunter Mr. J. Goodman. One day, a package turned up at our laboratory. It contained grainy film footage of a huge, ape-like creature and a scrawled note: *Bluff Creek, California. There are plenty more out there!* I was at once asked to investigate, a quest that took me across the rough terrain of northwest America and Canada.

April 24, Bluff Creek

I have set up camp in a lonely clearing near the creek. Last night, I was awakened by the sound of snapping wood, and this morning found some huge tree branches lying around. While walking earlier today, I suddenly became aware of a truly horrible smell. I feel certain that something was watching me through the trees...

April 29

Success at last! This afternoon, I came across some enormous footprints and found tufts of reddish fur caught on tree bark. Walking back to camp, I was startled to hear a high-pitched shriek. I suppose it is possible that it was a mountain lion—or was it a bigfoot?

Smells like rotting meat and flowers

Check fur tuft against color of local bears

Track is like a giant human's

Footprint cast–almost 2 feet (61cm) long!

Note: long fingers and sharp nails

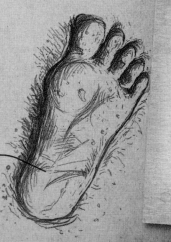

Note: extremely broad heel

Vital statistics

Name:	Bigfoot; Sasquatch
Height:	10–13 feet (3–4m)
Description:	Hairy; giant feet; foul-smelling
Call:	Spine-tingling shrieks
Diet:	Wild berries and nuts; known to steal peanut-butter sandwiches
Behavior:	Reserved; may throw rocks if provoked

Bigfoot Study

High forehead suggests intelligence

Deep-set eyes

BIGFOOT IN THE FLESH

Despite many weeks of searching at Bluff Creek, it was not until my hunt moved to the Canadian wilderness that I finally witnessed a bigfoot with my own eyes. I had almost given up hope of ever seeing one, and was in fact photographing a moose, when a monster ape stepped out from behind a pine tree and hurled a rock at me. I turned to run, though luckily the bottom part of the beast was caught on camera.

Canine teeth found at Bluff Creek— very similar to a gorilla's!

THE YETI

I had long heard tales of the yeti, the ape-like monster said to stalk the Himalayan Mountains. However, it was not until I read an intriguing newspaper article about an explorer's strange encounter with this beast that I decided to journey to Tibet.

Is there more than one yeti species?

MOUNTAINEER RESCUED BY YETI

LHASA. A mountaineer who was missing for a period of five days has claimed that he owes his survival to the yeti. Captain Murray-Hill, who was attempting to scale Mount Everest, says he became separated from his companions during a fierce blizzard. He was nearing death from exposure, when a shaggy, ape-like figure appeared and dragged him off to a cave.

His next memory is of waking alone in the same cave, seemingly recovered and with the strength to descend to safety.

Vital statistics

Name:	The yeti; the Abominable Snowman
Height:	10–12 feet (3–3.7m)
Description:	Ape-like body; white, shaggy fur
Call:	Unearthly yowl
Diet:	Yaks; sheep; foraged plants
Behavior:	Unpredictable; shy yet curious

White fur allows the yeti to blend in with a snowy landscape

Sharp fangs— definitely a meat-eater!

The yeti's human-like hands.

Toes are clawed

TALES FROM TIBET

Once in Tibet, I made contact with several local people who claimed either to have seen huge footprints or to have encountered the beast they call the "wild mountain man." One Sherpa girl, who had been tending her yaks, described how a huge white ape suddenly appeared and attempted to drag her away. When she screamed, the creature released her, but savagely attacked and killed one of her animals.

GIANT FOOTPRINTS

Puzzled by differing accounts of the yeti, I managed to track down two guides willing to lead me up towards the frozen mountain peaks. On the second night of our ascent, a snowstorm gathered force. As we lay in our tent, I was almost certain I could hear a strange yowling through the wind. Stepping out the following morning, I saw a huge, shadowy figure lumbering away through the mist. I ran to the spot—and sure enough, found giant footprints in the snow. My terrified guides would take me no farther, however, and I had no choice but to return with them to base camp.

HALF HUMANS

Many of the world's most horrifying beasts have human features. Those venturing into jungles must watch out for the man-eating manticore. With a human head, a lion's body, three rows of savage teeth, and a deadly dragon's tail, this creature may briefly be mistaken for a very short man. Across southern Europe, beware of the screeching harpies! With women's faces and vultures' bodies, these clawed beasts swoop down from the skies to snatch food.

Harpy Study

Huge talons

The manticore

The terrible smell that follows the harpies around serves as a warning that they are nearby.

Minotaur Study

This ancient Minotaur horn is believed to have dark magical powers.

PART MAN, PART BULL

The ancient Greeks told of the ferocious Minotaur, a terrifying creature that was part man, part bull. Thankfully now extinct, this bellowing monster was kept at the center of a maze by King Minos of Crete. Every nine years, 14 young men and women were sacrificed to the beast to satisfy its craving for human flesh. Eventually, the Athenian hero Theseus ended the terror by slaying the monster in its lair.

THE GORGONS

It was while traveling through Greece that I first had the opportunity to study those snake-haired monsters known as the Gorgons. By chance, I struck up a conversation with an old fisherman on the island of Serifos. When the man discovered my profession, he told me that he could lead me to the Gorgons' secret lair.

Hair of venomous snakes

A half-serpent gorgon

A pack of limbed gorgons

A deadly gaze

A DEADLY GAZE

I was somewhat alarmed, for all monster trackers know that the Gorgons are among the most deadly of beasts. Legend tells that one glance alone from their staring eyes is enough to turn any creature to stone! However, the chance to prove their existence could not be missed, and so the following day I boarded the man's boat.

A mouse turned to stone.

Vital statistics

Name:	Gorgon
Description:	Very ugly; hypnotic eyes; serpent hair
Call:	Loud hissing (from hair region)
Diet:	Human organs
Behavior:	Cunning; without mercy

Gorgon Study

Snake skin from the Gorgons' lair.

The Gorgons are
no beauty queens!

A mirror is essential for the
safe viewing of Gorgons.

July 19, near Serifos

We are sailing west in a boat named the Medusa. My companion only smiles mysteriously when I enquire as to our whereabouts. However, he has given me a small mirror and told me that, should we come upon a Gorgon, I should look only at the creature's reflection—otherwise I might meet a stony end!

July 20

Late this afternoon, we arrived on a rocky and seemingly deserted island. My guide led the way to a damp, eerie cave. No Gorgons appeared to be present, but I was horrified to see several figures of people and animals that had been turned to stone. I removed a mouse as evidence, as well as scraps of what appears to be snake skin.

Snake skin has a strange glow—magical powers?

MIXED-UP MONSTERS

Some of the world's most nightmarish beasts are those made up of different animal parts. In Egypt, Ammut—or "the Devourer"—has the head of a crocodile, the front body of a tiger, and the back body of a hippopotamus. The fire-breathing chimera possesses a lion's head, a goat's head rising from its back, and a serpent's head at the end of its tail. Like a dragon, this beast scorches its prey and may also poison victims with a single bite from its deadly tail.

Vicious-looking monkey's head

28

Caution:
if the nue catches sight of you, it will almost certainly bring you bad luck!

Fearsome tiger claws

THE TERRIBLE NUE

Sometimes referred to as the "Japanese chimera," the nue may be found hiding out in mountainous regions. This horrible creature has a monkey's head, a stout raccoon-like body, the legs of a tiger, and a viper's tail. When threatened, the beast may transform itself into a black cloud. The nue is very seldom seen, which is fortunate, for it is the bringer of bad luck. It is for this reason that the creature has only rarely been studied, although fascinating evidence has been gathered from its habitat.

Chimera

Ammut

Horrible Hounds

Huge, snarling watchdogs are known to guard the underworld realms of the dead. Cerberus is the three-headed monster found at the entrance to Hades, the Greek underworld. Although any soul may enter this terrifying place, all are prevented from leaving. The ferocious Garm watches over the Norse place of the dead, known as Helheim. It is said that the bloodcurdling howl of this four-eyed hound will one day signal the end of the world.

Black Dogs

Across the world, the sight of a black phantom hound is a sign that bad luck is close at hand. This beast's coat is blacker than night, and its giant paws don't make a sound as it moves. Most terrifying of all, though, are the creature's eyes, which blaze like hot coals. Black dogs commonly haunt places such as crossroads and graveyards; witnesses often report feeling a sudden chill just before seeing them. It is therefore advisable that if you experience sudden goose bumps while out walking at night, you should quickly change direction.

CERBERUS

The story of how Heracles wrestled with Cerberus, the three-headed guardian of the Greek underworld, is well known, although I had always assumed the tale was little more than a legend. However, while visiting the southernmost tip of the Greek mainland, a guide offered to show me the "gate to Hades."

GUARDIAN OF THE UNDERWORLD

The watery cave said to lead down to Hades can only be reached by boat, and my guide, Adrian, insisted that the trip should be made after nightfall. We set off in a small rowboat, and an hour or so later, a deep cavern loomed before us. The water glistened eerily at the entrance, but ahead lay only blackness. I shivered as Adrian steered the boat into the cave, for the ancient Greeks wrote of how Cerberus permitted none to leave his terrifying realm.

The Greek hero Heracles once wrestled with Cerberus.

Front-paw Study

Very sharp claws

Enormous pads

Cerberus Study

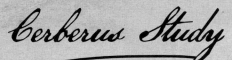

Vital statistics

Name: Cerberus
Description: Three-headed hound; glowing red eyes
Call: Spine-chilling barks and snarls
Diet: Passing strangers
Behavior: Ever-watchful; prone to gnashing teeth

A ferocious bite

A massive fang found at the cave entrance.

Each of Cerberus's three savage heads will feed only on living meat

January 21, Cape Tainaron, Greece

After a few moments, Adrian stopped rowing and pointed to a large opening in the rock face ahead. Silently, I clambered from the vessel and swiftly gathered evidence. Once I was safely back in the boat, Adrian uttered the following words in a commanding voice:

Oh, Hound of Hades, your lair is found
Where dead souls enter underground.

From just above our heads came a ferocious snarl and a terrible gnashing of teeth. It was clear that we were in mortal danger. Adrian began to row away quickly. I forced myself to glance back—and saw six red eyes burning through the blackness.

BEASTS *of the* EARTH

·ᴥ· R A R E ·ᴥ·
SPECIMENS

a collection of
TEETH, CLAWS, and OTHER CURIOSITIES
*discovered on expeditions
to the far-flung corners of the Earth*

ABOVE *This giant troll tooth
was found near human remains
in a deep forest-burrow.*

ABOVE *Scaly skin taken
from the dragon-like tail of
the deadly manticore.*

ABOVE *Found near the peak
of Mount Everest, this fang is
almost certainly a yeti's.*

LEFT *This hooked harpy claw, discovered in Greece, is the only known specimen of its kind.*

LEFT *This clump of bigfoot fur was discovered caught on tree bark at Bluff Creek, California.*

ABOVE *This nue claw is kept in a sealed chest. Any who touch it are likely to have bad fortune.*

RIGHT *A piece of horn from the chimera's goat-like head.*

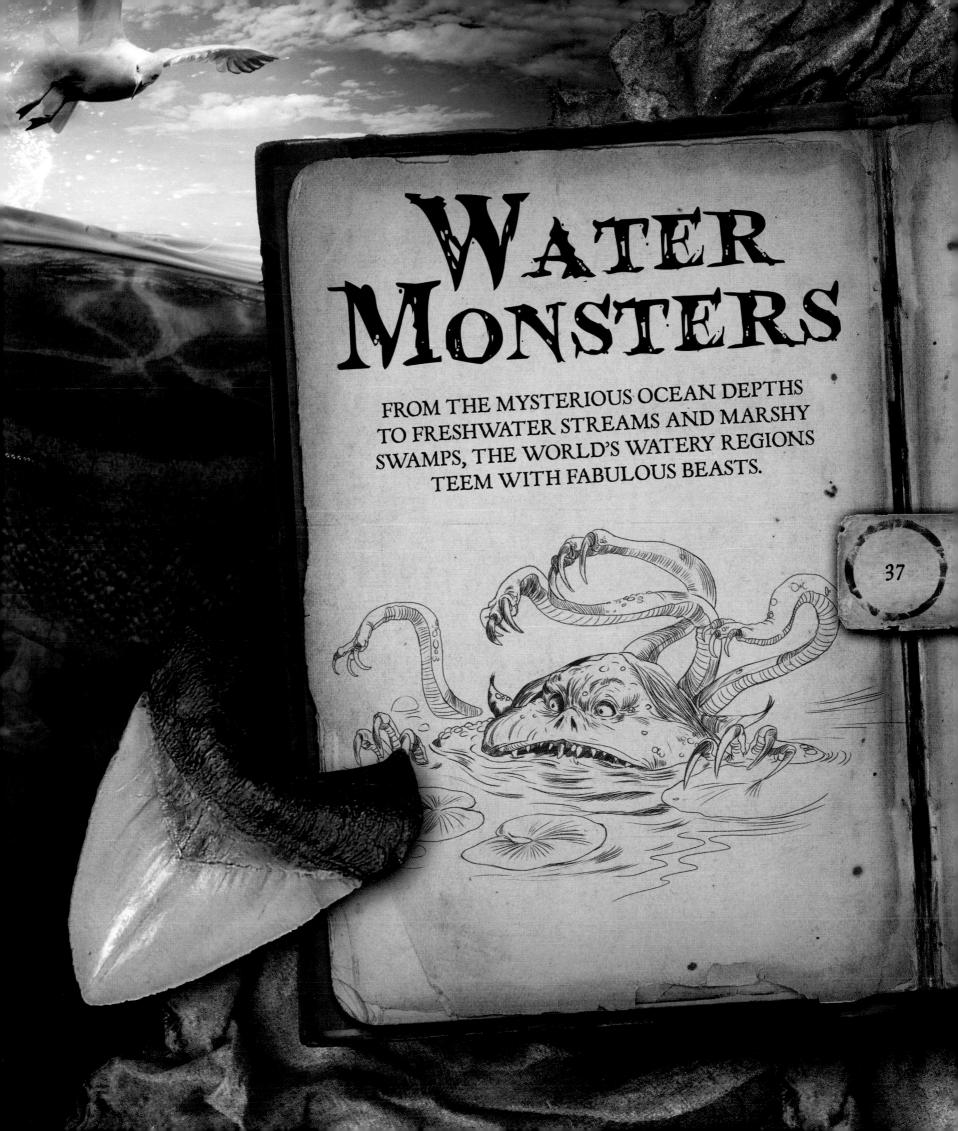

WATER MONSTERS

FROM THE MYSTERIOUS OCEAN DEPTHS TO FRESHWATER STREAMS AND MARSHY SWAMPS, THE WORLD'S WATERY REGIONS TEEM WITH FABULOUS BEASTS.

WATER SERPENTS

The curse of both seas and freshwater lakes, powerful water serpents lurk within seemingly calm waters. With massively long bodies, these beasts possess gaping jaws lined with razor-sharp teeth. Most move like land snakes, although some have paddle-like limbs. When excited, these creatures are capable of creating enormous waves, although they are known for the stealthy manner in which they can slide through water, creating barely a ripple. Passing boats and unsuspecting swimmers are sucked down swiftly and usually consumed whole.

A jagged lake-serpent tooth found washed ashore.

WAITING AND WATCHING

It is often said that water serpents are "shy" due to their habit of staying hidden from view, but "crafty" is probably a better description. Indeed, these creatures are capable of lying motionless for hours at a time, and may be mistaken for floating logs. An exception to this is the sea serpent of Cape Ann, Massachusetts, in North America, which hundreds have claimed to have seen over the years. On the other hand, the Loch Ness Monster of Scotland has been witnessed much less frequently and appears to be most active late at night.

Venemous barbs are found on the tails of some species

The Southern Ocean is home to a rare and deadly sea serpent with a lion-like head.

THE LOCH NESS MONSTER

O ne of my first tasks as a young beast hunter was to seek out the world-famous Loch Ness Monster of Scotland. At the time, there had been several recent sightings of this strangely elusive creature, although it was the account of a doctor— who claimed he had seen the monster *out* of water—that caught my attention.

The waters of Loch Ness are incredibly deep and dark

Dagger-like teeth

It was around midnight when I set out on the road along the north shore of Loch Ness. I was suddenly aware of a great commotion up ahead and was shocked to see an enormous creature crashing through the undergrowth, a deer hanging from its jaws. There followed an almighty splash as the beast disappeared.

I can only describe this "animal" as serpent-like, although it appeared to have flippers. If you would care to venture up to these parts, I would happily show you the exact spot.

Yours sincerely,
Dr. Russell McLean

An early photograph of Nessie.

Loch Ness Monster Study

Four powerful flippers

FINDING NESSIE

I set up camp around the ancient castle ruins overlooking the loch. After several weeks of seeing nothing, I was awakened one night by splashing and the terrified shout of a man. Leaping from my tent, I saw a flurry of movement out on the water before I realized that I was looking at an enormous "hump." Within seconds, it had sunk from view and the loch was perfectly still. The next day, I learned that a fisherman had disappeared; he was never seen again, although a week later a few wooden boat fragments—one scarred with what looked like tooth marks—were washed ashore.

Boat wood showing large tooth marks.

LOCAL FISHERMAN MISSING ON LOCH NESS

Vital statistics

Name:	Loch Ness Monster, Nessie
Description:	Snake-like body; paddle-like limbs
Call:	Stealthily silent
Diet:	Large animals; may swallow boats whole
Behavior:	Nocturnal; secretive; greedy

INVERNESS—Police are investigating the mysterious disappearance of a night

A tourist camping in the castle grounds claims to have heard loud splashing and

THE HYDRA

The legend of the terrifying Hydra and how the Greek hero Heracles cut off its nine heads has always fascinated me. Imagine my astonishment when a letter arrived from the Greek village of Myloi—a place close to the swamp where the Hydra once lived—urgently requesting the assistance of a monster expert.

Deadly breath kills victims instantly

As you must know, one of the Hydra's nine heads was immortal, and Heracles buried this still-living head beneath a great boulder. Unfortunately, this ancient grave seems to have been disturbed, for poisonous fumes are rising up from the ground and all who pass are troubled by a dreadful hissing. We are in need of your help!

DEADLY POISON

Excited by the possibility of coming face to face with the Hydra's still-living head, I made plans at once to travel to the area. Before setting off, however, I studied the ancient writings of the great monster hunters to ensure I was prepared. There had been many before me who had sought to find the Hydra's head in the hope of bottling the beast's poison. I also learned that it would be wise to take along a magical musical instrument, useful for charming serpents.

Vital statistics

Name:	The Hydra
Description:	Once a nine-headed serpent; now much reduced
Call:	A terrifying hiss
Diet:	May go for long periods without eating
Behavior:	Attention-seeking; hungry

THE IMMORTAL HEAD

Hydra Study

Upon arriving in Greece, I discovered that several people had already attempted to investigate the suspected burial site, but none had returned. A guide led me part of the way, then pointed at some distant rocks. Wearing a protective mask, I walked towards the stones and glanced into a hissing pit. Sure enough, there was the writhing head of a serpent, its burning eyes fixed upon me. I began to play my pipe and the creature soon fell into a trance. After I'd made some sketches and bottled the Hydra's breath, I heaved several boulders over the hole.

The Hydra once had nine hungry heads—thankfully just one remains

To those who seek the Hydra's head
Be most afraid and filled with dread!
This beast has neither strength nor claws
But poisonous breath in deadly jaws!

From the ancient writings of Cornelius Quail

A beast-charming pipe.

SEA MONSTERS

Throughout the ages, sailors have feared the strange and fantastical creatures that lurk beneath the ocean waves. Some sea monsters slither silently through the water like deadly snakes, while others rise from the depths to crush ships with giant tentacles and gaping jaws. Other beasts, like the fearsome Scylla, hide out in sea caves, watching for passing vessels. When one passes too close to Scylla's cliff-side lair, the monster's six snarling heads dart out to snatch victims.

The all-seeing eye of an Arctic sea monster.

Making a serious study of giant sea beasts can be a dangerous task.

THE SINGING SIRENS

On rocky islands dotted throughout the oceans live the bewitching sirens. These sea nymphs have the upper bodies of women and the lower bodies of birds, and at first glance appear rather beautiful. Beware, however, for the sirens possess vicious fangs behind their pretty faces! Many sailors have been lured to their deaths by the sound of these creatures singing. When passing nearby, it is advisable to block your ears in some fashion, for the sirens' voices cast a spell that is almost impossible to resist.

Scylla

A clawed mermaid

A dragon-tailed sea beast

"...they writhed gasping as Scylla swung them up her cliff and there at her cavern's mouth she bolted them down raw..."

A description of Scylla in Homer's Odyssey

THE KRAKEN

Of all the terrifying beasts that lurk beneath the waves, it is only the kraken that fills me with dread. This squid-like monster is so enormous that some unfortunate souls have mistaken its vast body for an island. When the time came to make a detailed study of this creature, I realized I must turn to the ancient wisdom of the great monster hunters for guidance.

Kraken Study

Krakens only rise from the icy depths to feed

GRASPING TENTACLES

Before my crew and I set sail in our research vessel, the *Hippocamp*, I carefully studied the many stories of ships being dragged down by a kraken's enormous tentacles. However, some experts claimed that the monster actually preferred eating other sea monsters to humans. It was only if a ship happened to be passing that the vessel—and its crew—would be sucked down and consumed.

The kraken's immense tentacles are strong enough to sink ships.

It has been observed that krakens are only ever found in waters more than 80 fathoms deep. If a depth measurement suddenly and inexplicably falls below 30 fathoms, then you may assume—with some certainty—that a kraken is lurking beneath your vessel!

Muscular tongue

An extract from Fantastic Beasts of the Seven Seas by Professor A. Koken

Vital statistics

Name: *The kraken*
Description: *Squid-like; massively long tentacles*
Call: *Mournful wails*
Diet: *Sea serpents; whales; people (in order of preference)*
Behavior: *High and mighty; inconsiderate*

Eight massively long tentacles are lined with powerful suckers

A Giant Whirlpool

After several months at sea, we found ourselves just off the coast of Iceland. One still afternoon, the sea's depth measurement suddenly plummeted and I realized we were in great peril. Sailing rapidly south, we anchored at what we hoped was a safe distance and waited anxiously. Soon, the sea began to toss and swell, and a giant, slimy mass broke through the waves. Massive, writhing tentacles stretched out from the body, grasping for prey, and almost reached our vessel. Then, this incredible "island" sank from sight, and with it, millions of fish—as well as some larger unidentified creatures—were sucked down into a raging whirlpool.

The suckers trap prey

FRESHWATER BEASTS

The rivers, lakes, and swamps of the world are home to a startling variety of fearsome beasts. Small children and animals that stray too near to the water's edge are at particular risk from some of these creatures. However, all must take care, for it is a sad fact that many adults have vanished in mysterious circumstances while taking a riverside stroll or going for a quick swim.

Bunyip tusk

Bunyip Study

LYING IN WAIT

Hidden beneath bridges or submerged just below the water's surface, hideous water trolls lie in wait for their prey. These creatures are always hungry and will snatch victims at every opportunity. The less common gryndylow is found in bogs or lakes, and occasionally even in ponds. This fearsome little creature uses octopus-like tentacles to grasp its prey. In Australia, the terrible man-eating bunyip hides out in swamps and creeks. Although hardly ever seen, this beast's presence is certainly felt at night, when its bloodcurdling howls may be heard from a great distance.

Very few have seen the bunyip and lived to tell the tale

Gryndylow Study

Exceptional eyesight

Tentacles can sense the tiniest movement

Kelpie Study

THE KELPIE

The mysterious kelpie is a beautiful horse seen wandering along the banks of rivers and lakes. The creature appears to be lost, and many have made the mistake of mounting its sleek back, for the horse nuzzles those who approach it and has gentle eyes. However, any who attempt to ride it are doomed, for they become stuck fast and cannot escape. The kelpie then gallops off at speed and plunges into deep water, carrying its unfortunate victim down to a silent grave.

The kelpie's gentle appearance hides a dark nature

A kelpie's hoofprint.

WATER MONSTERS

RARE SPECIMENS

a collection of
TEETH, TUSKS, and OTHER CURIOSITIES
*found on expeditions to the
world's water regions*

ABOVE *A shark-like tooth found washed up on the shore of Loch Ness in Scotland.*

RIGHT *Horned sea monsters are a rare but deadly presence in the world's oceans.*

ABOVE *The bunyip uses its curved tusks to heave itself onto dry land and "hook" passersby.*

LEFT *This skin fragment from an unidentified sea monster is tougher than a rhinoceros hide.*

RIGHT *The serrated tooth of a water serpent encountered in the icy depths of the Arctic Ocean.*

ABOVE *The enlarged eyes of the gryndylow allow this beast to detect prey in very dark water.*

RIGHT *A tentacle segment, cut from a huge sea beast as it attempted to drag down a boat.*

BEASTS OF THE AIR

THE SKIES ABOVE US ARE HOME TO
A MULTITUDE OF WINGED WONDERS,
FROM MAJESTIC, FEATHERED BIRD-BEASTS
TO FIRE-BREATHING DRAGONS.

Half Bird Half Beast

T he skies are filled with a host of incredible bird-beasts. Since they are so seldom seen by human eyes, it is thought that these creatures somehow occupy a different realm—one that only occasionally merges with the world we see.

Terrifying Bird-Monsters

The giant griffin has the head, wings, and talons of an eagle but the hindquarters of a lion. This powerful creature is well known for its habit of stealing gold and precious stones, and guarding such treasures in its mountain nest. In Africa, the much-feared roc glides over the open plains in search of prey. Elephants are the roc's first choice of food, though it will readily swoop down to snatch other large creatures, including humans.

Reptile scales start to appear underneath the neck feathers

Cockatrice Study

Rooster wings combine with clawed "hands"

Griffin

THE COCKATRICE

A few years ago, I happened to meet Dr. da'Costa, a well-known scientist carrying out research on European toads. When he told me that one of the reptiles under his watch had been behaving very oddly—in short, guarding a large egg from an unknown creature—I immediately guessed that the egg might contain a deadly cockatrice. As all monster hunters know, this rare beast is the product of a cockerel's egg laid on the stroke of midnight, then incubated by a toad or serpent.

Dragon tail

The egg must be tended by a toad or snake before it can hatch.

June 14, Black Craw Woods

Avoid beast's eyes at all cost!

Since the toad has been guarding the egg for many months, I feel sure the cockatrice may hatch at any moment. I carry a small mirror (for turning the beast's deadly gaze back upon itself) and a caged weasel. This animal is the cockatrice's sworn enemy and should protect me.

June 23

When I came to look at the egg this morning, the toad was hopping about excitedly. The shell began to crack and a truly extraordinary creature wriggled free. I can only describe it as half rooster, half reptile. I stayed well out of its sight, though the toad was not so lucky, for the poor animal fell over stone dead.

Must find a way to bottle the beast's scorching breath

THE HIPPOGRIFF

The majestic hippogriff is the offspring of a griffin and a horse. Since griffins and horses are sworn enemies, the hippogriff is a rare beast indeed. Although I have been fortunate enough to witness griffins on several occasions, I longed to set eyes on a hippogriff more than anything.

A RARE DISCOVERY

A few years ago, I spent several months studying the nesting habits of North African griffins. One afternoon, I scrambled up a steep gully to examine a nest. Expecting to see several griffin eggs and perhaps some jewels, I was instead amazed to find a single golden egg. With great excitement, I realized it must surely contain a baby hippogriff.

Head is that of a great eagle, both cruel and majestic

Sleek and sturdy horse's body

A truly majestic sight!

Could a hippogriff ever be tamed?

October 17
Today, I finally witnessed the incredible sight of a young hippogriff as it took its first flight. What a marvelous creature it is!

November 12
The hippogriff frequently prowls the mountains alone, and I am tracking it daily. I believe it is slowly getting used to my presence, although it sometimes seems startled to see me and swiftly takes to the skies.

November 18
Today, the hippogriff took from my outstretched hand the gift of a dead rabbit. I am beginning to dream that in time it might actually allow me to climb onto its back...

Hooked beak for ripping through prey

Hind legs have a powerful kick

Hippogriff Study

Hippogriff talon

Vital statistics

Name:	Hippogriff
Description:	Part horse, part eagle; massive talons; glowing eyes
Call:	Loud squawks; may whinny
Diet:	Small mammals; grazes on grass
Behavior:	Noble; loyal; may attack if startled

Talons may reach 1 foot (30cm) in length

Immensely strong wings

Hippogriff feather

LIGHTNING SPEED

For a few weeks, I brought the hippogriff daily gifts of rabbits or mice. On one such occasion, the beast suddenly knelt down as if to encourage me to climb onto its back. Although much afraid, I grasped its feathered neck and pulled myself up. The hippogriff began to gallop, and then in a flash we were soaring over mountains at lightning speed. It is hard to describe the experience now, for it seems like a dream. Indeed, I could believe it *was* a dream, but for the fact that I still have a beautiful feather that came away in my hand.

DRAGONS

Ferocious, cunning, and wise, dragons are among the mightiest of beasts. Some soar majestically through the skies, while others slither serpent-like through rivers and lakes. Rare dragons may be found in the most extreme places. Volcanic dragons lay their eggs in bubbling lava while snow dragons make their lairs in frozen ice caves.

Wings are thin yet amazingly strong

DRAGON FIRE

As well as having dagger-sharp fangs and claws strong enough to cut through diamonds, most dragons possess the extraordinary ability to breathe scorching flames of fire. A single blast almost always results in instant death for the victim. For this reason, only experienced monster hunters should ever attempt to track dragons.

MAGIC AND MYSTERY

Many parts of the dragon are known to possess powerful magic. Those brave enough to consume a dead dragon's heart will discover that this feast gives them the ability to see into the future, while eating a dragon's enormous tongue can bring great wisdom. Ground horns and bones can be used to cure various illnesses, while dragon scales may bring good luck in the right hands. The most powerful part of a dragon, though, is its blood. Wizards will go to great lengths to find this incredible substance for their spells.

Skin is often extremely gnarled in appearance

Almost all lairs have
a treasure hoard

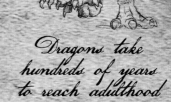

Dragons take
hundreds of years
to reach adulthood

Aged dragons
have incredible wisdom

Dragon fire may be bottled
by experienced beast hunters.

Of dragon blood I thee implore
To heed these words from ancient lore.

Drink it, and you will fathom the speech of birds
But spill it, and you will lose the power of words.

Treasure it, and you will find the dragon's hoard
But lose it, and you will perish by the sword.

BEASTS of the AIR

❧ RARE ❧ SPECIMENS

a collection of
EGGS, TALONS, and OTHER CURIOSITIES
*found on expeditions
around the world*

ABOVE *This claw of the rare
Arabian sand dragon has
hooked talons for seizing prey.*

BELOW *An enormous roc
talon, discovered near the
remains of an African elephant.*

ABOVE *This dragon egg,
discovered in volcanic lava,
is still warm to the touch.*

ABOVE *Cockatrice talons may be ground down by sorcerers and used in powerful spells.*

ABOVE *The eagle-like skull of a baby hippogriff discovered near a griffin nest.*

RIGHT *Griffin feathers are valued for their magical powers, though caution is advised.*

CREATURES OF THE NIGHT

BEWARE WHEN NIGHT-TIME FALLS, FOR THE HOURS OF DARKNESS ARE HAUNTED BY A MULTITUDE OF TERRIFYING AND UNNATURAL BEASTS.

BLOODSUCKERS

Terrible creatures that suck the blood of the living haunt the hours of darkness. While human-like vampires are the most common of these bloodthirsty beasts, the dog-like chupacabra or "goat-sucker" is feared across the Americas and beyond.

THIRST FOR BLOOD

Although vampires may take various forms, they all share the need to feast on blood. Despite their human appearance, these beasts have superhuman strengths, such as the ability to see in darkness or move at lightning speed. Although some vampires make their homes in tombs and emerge only at night, others are able to blend into human society. However, they must constantly move on to avoid being noticed, for vampires are immortal and never age.

Sharpened fangs are essential for gripping a victim's neck.

fig. A.
Curved fang of tomb-dwelling vampire

fig. B.
Vampires living among humans still display very long canines

fig. C.
A broken tooth found embedded in a victim's neck

Bloodshot eyes

Vampire Study

THE CHUPACABRA

Over the years, I had read various reports of the ferocious chupacabra. This beast was said to prefer goats' blood, and would leave its victims almost totally intact with just a few puncture wounds. When I received a letter from a farmer in Puerto Rico pleading for assistance, I decided it was time to investigate.

Chupacabra Study

Glowing eyes

Blood may seep from the mouth

Paws leave no tracks — extraordinary!

Garlic may be used to ward off vampires.

Night after night, some dreadful beast is killing our goats. Traps have been set and I lock my animals up, but each morning several goats lie dead with barely a mark on their poor bodies. I am beginning to fear for my own life!

I am almost certain this beast has super- natural powers

May 24, Puerto Rico

I am staying with Mr. Nacho López on his farm at the edge of the rain forest. I have been sleeping by day and keeping watch by night, but so far nothing — although the night is filled with eerie sounds and I am often afraid.

May 30

As I lay hidden tonight, I was suddenly aware of two red lights moving through the darkness — they must have been eyes. Next, the locked barn door creaked open, and I heard a quick flurry of movement. When I looked, three goats lay quite dead, each with an identical neck wound. Strangely, there were no tracks at all, though I did find what looks like a large claw...

How does this creature drain its victims of blood?

The Werewolf

Early in my monster-hunting career, a letter from Russia turned up at our research laboratory. The sender, one Selina Babikov, suspected her husband was a werewolf. It was agreed that, posing as a distant relative, I would travel to spend a few days with the couple.

My husband works as a woodcutter. About a year ago, he came home with scratches on his arm. He claimed they came from a wolf.

Since then, I have frequently awakened in the night to find him gone from the house. His clothes are sometimes torn, and I once found scraps of raw meat in his pockets. I have noticed, too, that his face seems more bristly and sometimes his eyes have a strange light.

Eyes keep their human intelligence

The Beast Within

Selina and her husband, Yuri, welcomed me warmly to their small house on the edge of a dense forest. I took great care that Yuri did not catch me observing him, but I immediately noticed several telltale signs: his eyebrows met in the middle, his fingernails were unusually long, and although I couldn't be sure, I thought I glimpsed a layer of hair under his tongue when we spoke.

Hands double in size, and nails turn into claws

Werewolf Study

Bones lengthen and muscle structure completely alters

Ripped clothing is often a telltale sign

Immensely powerful neck

Vital statistics

Name:	Werewolf; lycanthrope
Description:	In human form: hairy; in wolf form: glowing eyes, ferocious fangs
Call:	A bloodcurdling howl
Diet:	Raw meat, preferably human
Behavior:	Frenzied; ravenous

Could Yuri be "cured" of this curse?

How exactly does the moon cause this change?

November 27

The moon is not quite full, but Yuri seems restless. His eyes dart around and he seems unable to concentrate. At supper tonight, I was horrified to see him devouring a bloody steak in just a few mouthfuls.

November 29

Just after midnight, I heard a noise outside. Peering through the window, I saw Yuri stepping quickly towards the dark forest. The man looked up at the full moon and then let out an unearthly howl. His hands began to claw at his clothes, fangs erupted from his jaws, and fur seemed to cover his body. And then this terrible wolf-beast disappeared into the trees...

Werewolf transformation

The change from man to beast must be very painful!

A bite from a wild wolf may pass on the werewolf curse.

ZomBies

Rotting corpses brought back to life by witchcraft stalk the land of the living. Often called the "undead," zombies have no minds of their own and are servants to the sorcerers who summoned them back from the grave. Pale and bloodless, they may be identified by their lumbering walk and horrible stench. Beware of finding one on your trail, though, for zombies have a taste for human flesh and will never give up on a task they have been instructed to perform!

The Living Dead

Powerful sorcerers use spells to snatch up the souls of the dead and lock them in bottles. These unlucky souls are then instructed to bring their own dead bodies back to life. It is a difficult job to get rid of a zombie's attention, for these creatures feel no pain. Your only hope is to find and smash the bottle containing the zombie's soul, or somehow to trick your undead companion into eating salt. This should send a zombie straight back to its grave.

ALIENS

It seems likely that beings from outer space are living right here on Earth, although some experts claim that aliens are only occasional visitors to our planet. "Grays," with their enlarged heads and huge, almond-shaped eyes, are the most commonly spotted extraterrestrials. They are most likely to be seen in remote areas at night, emerging from their spacecraft. You would be advised to steer clear of these sinister beings, since they are well known for kidnapping people and performing strange experiments on them.

When observing spacecraft, great care must be taken to avoid kidnap.

Grays may be identified by their large, hairless heads.

It is believed that reptoids come from the constellation Draco.

Alien hands—very unhuman!

LIVING AMONG US

There are many clues to suggest that reptilian humans have been secretly living among us for thousands of years. Known as "reptoids," these alien creatures are thought to come from the constellation Draco. Reptoids are highly intelligent and are capable of appearing in many disguises, so it is quite possible that these disturbing beasts are more familiar than you may realize.

Preserved reptoid finger—note the slimy texture.

Reptoids are masters of disguise and are seldom seen in their natural "reptilian" form.

THE BOGEYMAN

I must confess that I had always assumed that the bogeyman was nothing more than an imaginary monster useful for frightening naughty children. Indeed, as a youngster I well remember fearing the horrible beast that surely lurked in the shadows of my bedroom. However, a strange experience a few years ago caused me to think again.

A CREEPY HOUSE

Family friends had rented an old house in the country and I was invited to join them for a few days. The house and grounds were large and rambling, the perfect place for youngsters to run around. However, I cannot forget the strange chill that hung heavy in the dimly lit rooms, or the unnerving creaks that seemed to echo around the house late at night.

Long, bony fingers

76

Only ever seen by children?

I wonder whether this monster even has a face?

August 12

At dinner tonight, Will was misbehaving and generally being nasty to his sister. His father told him that the bogeyman would pay him a visit if he didn't stop it immediately. I couldn't help noticing the look of sheer terror that crossed the child's face.

August 13

Late last night, I heard several screams. This morning, Will's parents told me he had suffered a nightmare—though the boy insisted he had been awake. He described hearing footsteps followed by scratching at the window. Petrified, he peeked through the curtains and glimpsed a huge cloaked figure. Only a hand was clearly visible: white and bony, with long curved nails.

Footprint is almost twice as large as an average man's

Nails like blades

ood covers face

STARTLING EVIDENCE

Not surprisingly, Will refused to sleep in the same room again, and the rest of the stay passed without further incident. However, the morning after the boy's "dream," I took a good look outside the bedroom and was startled to find very large footprints in the soil. There was also a series of deep scratches on the windowpane and I found a scrap of black material that had caught on the thorny bushes just below.

Could this be the face of the bogeyman?

Bogeyman Study

Abnormally long forearms

Animal skull pendant

Vital statistics	
Name:	*Bogeyman*
Description:	*Cloaked figure; long nails (rarely seen, presence usually "felt")*
Habitat:	*Under beds and in closets; just outside the bedroom window*
Behavior:	*Nasty; delights in terrifying children*

Torn material from the bogeyman's cloak

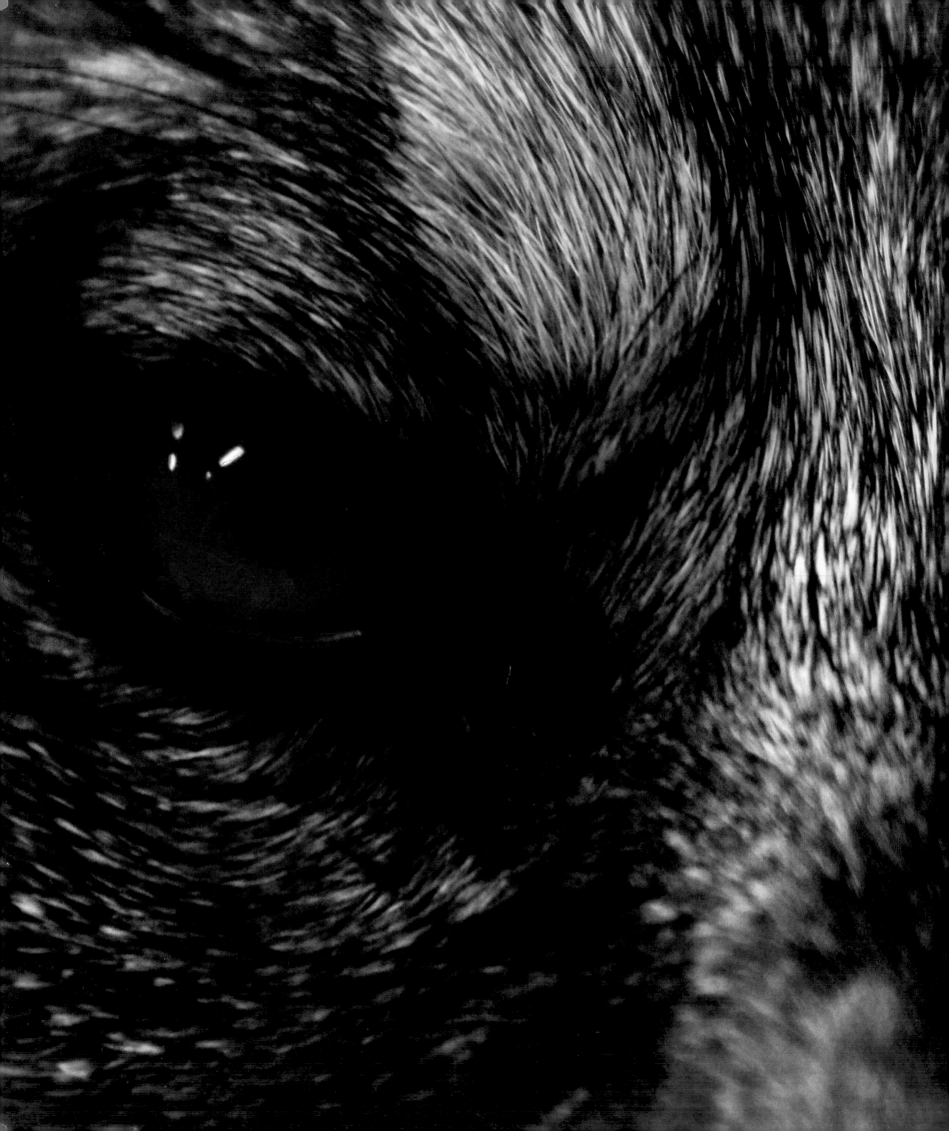

ACKNOWLEDGMENTS

During my long career studying the beasts of the world, I have learned much from the great monster hunters of ages past and present. They are too many to name here, but their knowledge and invaluable wisdom—often gained at considerable risk to their own safety—have been a constant source of inspiration to me.

In addition, I would like to extend my gratitude to all those who have made the writing and production of this book possible: my editor (and fellow beast enthusiast) Alex Koken; the designers Jake da'Costa and Russell Porter; Wild Pixel for Photoshop and CGI artwork; Leo Brown and Rebecca Wright for the illustrations; Paul Langan for picture research; and Charlotte Cade for production.

S. A. Caldwell

The publishers would like to thank the following sources for their kind permission to reproduce the pictures in this book. The page numbers for each of the photographs are listed below, giving the page on which they appear in the book and any location indicator (C-centre, T-top, B-bottom, L-left, R-right).

ALAMY: /Classic Image: 44B; /WENN Ltd: 51L

CORBIS: /Steve Kaufman: 35BR

FORTEAN PICTURE LIBRARY: /René Dahinden: 20C

GETTY IMAGES: /The British Library/Robana: 39C; /Dave Buresh/The Denver Post: 20TR; /DEA/G. Dagli Orti /De Agostini: 32BL; /Datacraft Co Ltd: 1, 36-37; /Dorling Kindersley: 43; /Robbie George/National Geographic: 58-59; /Frank Greenaway/Dorling Kindersley: 58-59; /John Hay: 16TR; /Maria Itina/Moment Open: 58-59; /Keystone: 40; /Dave King/Dorling Kindersley: 49C; /Jay M Pasachoff/Science Faction: 74BL; /Science & Society Picture Library: 39B

ISTOCKPHOTO.COM: 1, 2-3, 6-7, 12-13, 36-37, 52-53, 58-59, 64-65, 68-69, 71, 72-73, 75L, 75R, 77L

NATIONAL GEOGRAPHIC CREATIVE: /Steven Ruiter/Foto Natura/Mind: 58-59

SHUTTERSTOCK: 1, 4-5C, 5TL, 5TR, 9, 10-11, 14-15, 19TL, 19TR, 21BR, 22, 25, 27, 29, 30-31, 35TL, 36-37, 38-39, 41, 44TR, 46, 51BR, 55, 56, 57, 62TR, 63R, 65B, 67, 74TR, 74BR, 77BR, 78-79

THINKSTOCK: 16-17, 21R, 49B, 66

Every effort has been made to acknowledge correctly and contact the source and/or copyright holder of each picture and Carlton Books Limited apologises for any unintentional errors or omissions that will be corrected in future editions of this book.